PIANO • VOCAL • GUITAR

THE BEST BIG BAND SONGS EVER

**69 Of The Greatest Big Band Hits including: I'll Never Smile Again •
In The Mood • Long Ago (And Far Away) • Marie • Moonglow • Opus One •
Sentimental Journey • A String Of Pearls • A Sunday Kind Of Love • 12th Street Rag**

*Indexed in Song Finder
Ref. 782.42
Ferguson*

*Songs Indexed
in Song-Index 2/16/04
RC*

ISBN 0-7935-1214-X

HL® Hal Leonard Publishing Corporation
7777 West Bluemound Road P.O. Box 13819 Milwaukee, WI 53213

Copyright © 1986, 1991 by HAL LEONARD PUBLISHING CORPORATION
International Copyright Secured   All Rights Reserved

CONTENTS
THE BEST BIG BAND SONGS EVER

ALRIGHT, OKAY, YOU WIN

Words and Music by
SID WYCHE and MAYME WATTS

Moderately, with rhythm

AMONG MY SOUVENIRS

Words by EDGAR LESLIE
Music by HORATIO NICHOLLS

Slowly, With Expression

ANGRY

Words by DUDLEY MECUM
Music by JULES CASSARD,
HENRY BRUNIES and MERRIT BRUNIES

BALLIN' THE JACK

Words by JIM BURRIS
Music by CHRIS SMITH

First you put your two knees close up tight,___ Then you sway 'em to the left, then you

sway 'em to the right, Step a-round the floor kind of nice and light,___ Then you

BASIN STREET BLUES

Moderately

Words and Music by
SPENCER WILLIAMS

BLUE CHAMPAGNE

Words and Music by
GRADY WATTS, FRANK RYERSON & JIMMY EATON

Slowly

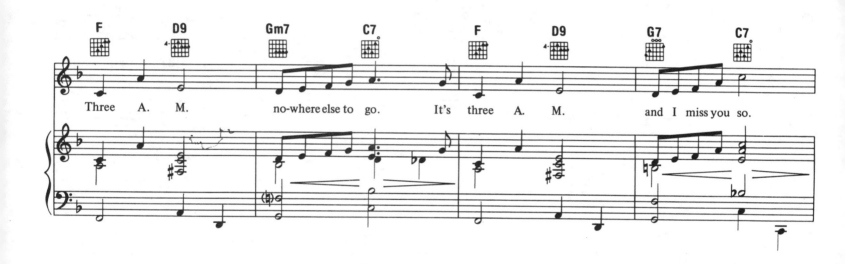

Three A. M. no-where else to go. It's three A. M. and I miss you so.

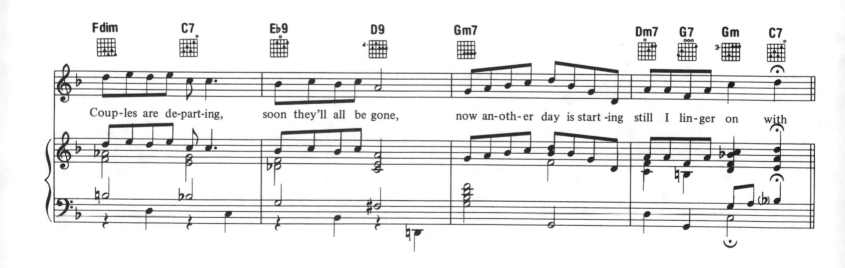

Coup-les are de-part-ing, soon they'll all be gone, now an-oth-er day is start-ing still I lin-ger on with

BOO-HOO

Words and Music by EDWARD HEY...
CARMEN LOMBARDO and JOHN JACOB LOEB

BOOGIE WOOGIE BUGLE BOY

Words and Music by
DON RAYE and HUGHIE PRINCE

Medium Boogie Woogie

He was a fa-mous trum-pet man from out Chi-

ca-go way, ___ He had a "boo-gie" style that no one

else could play. ___ He was the top man of his craft

BUGLE CALL RAG

By JACK PETTIS, BILLY MEYERS
and ELMER SCHOEBEL

© 1922, 1923 MILLS MUSIC, INC.
© Renewed 1950, 1951 EDWIN H. MORRIS & COMPANY, A Division of MPL Communications, Inc.
International Copyright Secured   All Rights Reserved

BYE BYE BLACKBIRD

Words by MORT DIXON
Music by RAY HENDERSON

CALDONIA
(WHAT MAKES YOUR BIG HEAD SO HARD?)

Words and Music by
FLEECIE MOORE

Medium boogie woogie tempo

don - ia! __ Cal - don - ia! __ What Makes Your Big Head So Hard?

CANDY

Words and Music by MACK DAVID,
JOAN WHITNEY and ALEX KRAMER

Moderately slow

CHERRY PINK AND APPLE BLOSSOM WHITE

French Words by JACQUES LARUE
English Words by MACK DAVID
Music by LOUIGUY

THE CONTINENTAL

Words by CON CONRAD
Music by HERBERT MAGIDSON

44

FIVE FOOT TWO, EYES OF BLUE
(HAS ANYBODY SEEN MY GIRL?)

Words by Joe Young and Sam Lewis
Music by Ray Henderson

Moderato

Laughed so loud I thought that I would cave in,
When we asked him for his wife's de - scrip - tion

When I heard that sil - ly, daf - fy - dil - ly rav - in':
He just an - swered all of us with this con - nip - tion:

Chorus, Moderato

Five Foot Two, Eyes Of Blue, But oh! what those five foot could do,___ Has

an - y - bod - y seen my girl?_____

Turned up nose, turned down hose, Nev - er had no oth - er beaus.___ Has

mp-mf

DADDY

Words and Music by
Bob Troup

Medium bounce tempo

Hey! lis - ten to my sto - ry 'bout_ a gal named Dai - sy Mae_ La - zy Dai - sy Mae_

Her dis-po - si - tion   is ra-ther sweet and charm-ing;

At times a - larm - ing.   So_ they   say. _____

(Interlude)

She had a

man rich, tall, dark, hand-some   large and strong to whom she used to sing this song:

52

DON'T GET AROUND MUCH ANYMORE

Words by BOB RUSSELL
Music by DUKE ELLINGTON

FOR SENTIMENTAL REASONS

Words by DEEK WATSON
Music by WILLIAM BEST

MCA music publishing

HARLEM NOCTURNE

Words by DICK ROGERS
Music by EARLE HAGEN

I CAN'T GIVE YOU ANYTHING BUT LOVE

Words by DOROTHY FIELDS
Music by JIMMY McHUGH

Moderately

G   G/B   Bbdim   Am7

I can't give you an-y-thing but love,

D7   G   G/B   Bbdim

Ba - by, ___ That's the on - ly thing I've plen - ty

Am7   D9   G7   C#dim

of, Ba - by. ___ Dream - in' a - while, ___

I'LL NEVER SMILE AGAIN

Words and Music by
RUTH LOWE

MCA music publishing

I'LL REMEMBER APRIL

Words and Music by DON RAYE,
GENE DE PAUL and PAT JOHNSON

I'M SITTING ON TOP OF THE WORLD

Allegro Moderato

Words by SAM M. LEWIS and JOE YOUNG
Music by RAY HENDERSON

IN THE MOOD

Words and Music by JOE GARLAND

INDIANA
(Back Home Again In Indiana)

Words by BALLARD MACDONALD
Music by JAMES F. HANLEY

Moderato

IN A LITTLE SPANISH TOWN
('Twas On A Night Like This)

Words by SAM M. LEWIS and JOE YOUNG
Music by MABEL WAYNE

Chorus, Slowly with much expression

In A Lit - tle Span - ish Town, 'Twas on a night like this,_____

Stars were peek - a - boo - ing down, 'Twas on a night like this,_____

I whis - pered "Be true to me,"_____ And she

sighed: "Si, Si."_____

IT'S A PITY TO SAY "GOODNIGHT"

Words and Music by
BILLY REID

JUNE NIGHT

Words by CLIFF FRIEND
Music by ABEL BAER

LEAP FROG

Music by JOE GARLAND

MCA music publishing

LET A SMILE BE YOUR UMBRELLA

Words by IRVING KAHAL
and FRANCIS WHEELER
Music by SAMMY FAIN

LET THERE BE LOVE

Lyric by IAN GRANT
Music by LIONEL RAND

LET'S DANCE

Words and Music by
FANNY BALDRIDGE, GREGORY STONE
and JOSEPH BONIME

LITTLE GIRL

Words and Music by MADELINE HYDE
and FRANCIS HENRY

Verse (ad lib.)

1. First time that I saw you as you went pass-ing by, I knew my search-ing days were through. Then I made my mind up that you would soon know why, That's when I start-ed tell-ing you:

2. I'm just bub-bling o-ver, my heart is thrill'd with pride, To think you're in my arms to-night. I'll be hap-py, al-ways with you right by my side, Each day a new dream of de-light;

Refrain (in tempo)

LIT-TLE GIRL, you're the one girl for me, LIT-TLE GIRL,

MCA music publishing

99

LONG AGO (AND FAR AWAY)

Words by IRA GERSHWIN
Music by JEROME KERN

Moderately Slow

MOONGLOW

Words and Music by
WILL HUDSON, EDDIE DeLANGE and IRVING MILLS

MAIRZY DOATS

By MILTON DRAKE, AL HOFFMAN,
and JERRY LIVINGSTON

107

MARIE
(From The Motion Picture "THE AWAKENING")

Words and Music by IRVING BERLIN

THE MOST BEAUTIFUL GIRL IN THE WORLD

(From "JUMBO")

Words by LORENZ HART
Music by RICHARD RODGERS

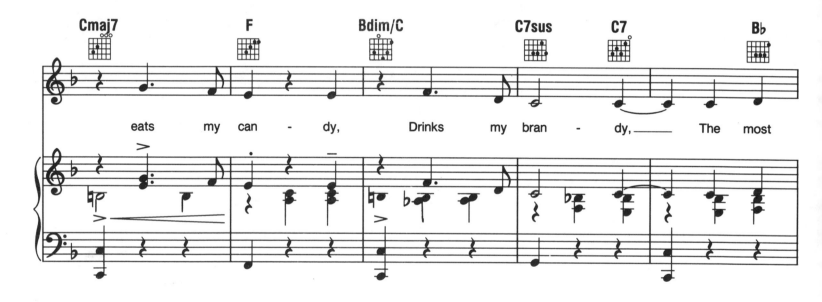

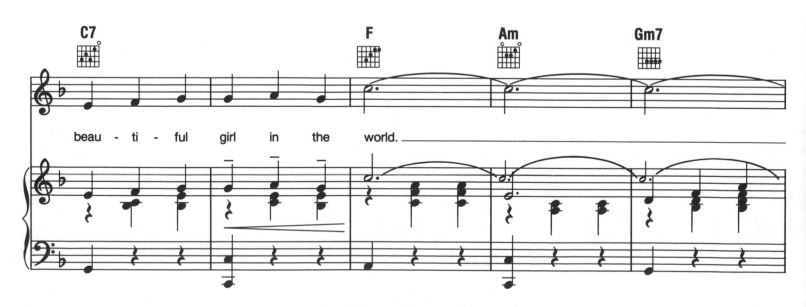

113

MY ROMANCE
(From "JUMBO")

Words by LORENZ HART
Music by RICHARD RODGERS

ris - ing in Spain, Nor a dance to a con-stant-ly sur-

pris - ing re - frain. Wide a - wake I can make my most fan-

tas - tic dreams come true; My ro - mance does-n't need a thing but

you. My ro -   you.

A NIGHTINGALE SANG IN BERKELEY SQUARE

Lyric by ERIC MASCHWITZ
Music by MANNING SHERWIN

OH! YOU BEAUTIFUL DOLL

Words by A. SEYMOUR BROWN
Music by NAT D. AYER

THE OLD LAMPLIGHTER

Words by Charles Tobias
Music by Nat Simon

ON A LITTLE STREET IN SINGAPORE

Words by BILLY HILL
Music by PETER De ROSE

ON THE SUNNY SIDE OF THE STREET

Lyric by DOROTHY FIELDS
Music by JIMMY McHUGH

134

OPUS ONE

Words and Music by
SY OLIVER

Moderate Jump Tempo

G I'm wrack-in' my brain, to think of a name, __ To give to this tune, so **C7**

A7 Per-ry can croon, __ And may-be Ol' Bing will give it a fling, __ And **Am7** **D9**

G **C#dim** that 'll start ev-'ry-one hum-min' the thing. __ **Am7** The mel-o-dy's dumb, **D9** **D9+5** **G** re-

SATIN DOLL

By DUKE ELLINGTON,
JOHNNY MERCER and BILLY STRAYHORN

SATURDAY NIGHT IS THE LONELIEST NIGHT OF THE WEEK

Words by SAMMY CAHN
Music by JULE STYNE

SEEMS LIKE OLD TIMES

Words and Music by JOHN JACOB LOEB
and CARMEN LOMBARDO

SENTIMENTAL JOURNEY

Words and Music by BUD GREEN,
LES BROWN and BEN HOMER

SOMEBODY LOVES YOU

Words by CHARLIE TOBIAS
Music by PETER DE ROSE

THE SHEIK OF ARABY

Words by HARRY B. SMITH
and FRANCIS WHEELER
Music by TED SNYDER

SOMEBODY ELSE IS TAKING MY PLACE

By DICK HOWARD, BOB ELLSWORTH
and RUSS MORGAN

SOMETIMES I'M HAPPY

Words by CLIFFORD GREY and LEO ROBIN
Music by VINCENT YOUMANS

A STRING OF PEARLS

Words by EDDIE DELANGE
Music by JERRY GRAY

Moderately Bright

SUNRISE SERENADE

Lyric by JACK LAWRENCE
Music by FRANKIE CARLE

SWEET SOMEONE

Words by GEORGE WAGGNER
Music by BARON KEYES

A SUNDAY KIND OF LOVE

Words and Music by BARBARA BELLE,
LOUIS PRIMA, ANITA LEONARD and STAN RHODES

MCA music publishing

UNDECIDED

Words by SID ROBIN
Music by CHARLES SHAVERS

MCA music publishing

174

TENDERLY

Lyric by JACK LAWRENCE
Music by WALTER GROSS

12TH STREET RAG

By EUDAY L. BOWMAN

Lively

The Way You Look Tonight

Words by DOROTHY FIELDS
Music by JEROME KERN

WHEN MY BABY SMILES AT ME

By HARRY VON TILZER, ANDREW B. STERLING,
BILL MUNRO and TED LEWIS

188

WHEN MY SUGAR WALKS DOWN THE STREET

With a beat

Words and Music by GENE AUSTIN,
JIMMIE McHUGH AND IRVING MILLS

I know a thing or two and I'm tell-ing you, I've got a won-der-ful

gal, She's got the cut-est smile, a mil-lion dol-lar style,

WHEN THE RED, RED ROBIN COMES BOB, BOB BOBBIN' ALONG

Words and Music by
HARRY WOODS

WHO?

Words by OTTO HARBACH and OSCAR HAMMERSTEIN II
Music by JEROME KERN

WHO'S SORRY NOW

Words by BERT KALMER & HARRY RUBY
Music by TED SNYDER

WRAP YOUR TROUBLES IN DREAMS
(And Dream Your Troubles Away)

Words by TED KOEHLER and BILLY MOLL
Music by HARRY BARRIS

YES INDEED

Words and Music by
SY OLIVER

With a Slow, measured beat

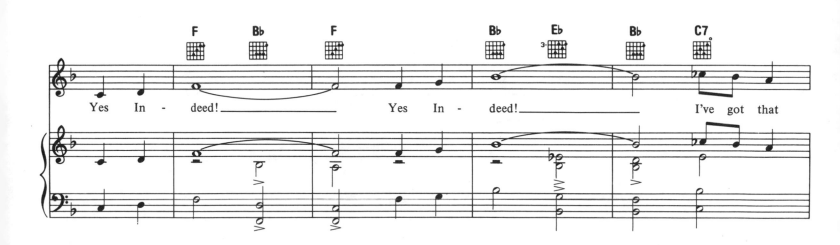

Yes In - deed!_____ Yes In - deed!_____ I've got that

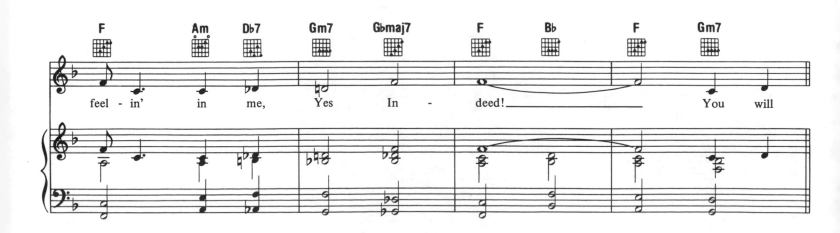

feel - in' in me, Yes In - deed!_____ You will

YESTERDAYS

Words by OTTO HARBACH
Music by JEROME KERN